Opinions About
The Trail of Tears
The Indian Removal Act

by Rebecca Grudzina and Joanne Tangorra

Table of Contents

Introduction

When Europeans arrived on the North American continent in the mid-fifteenth century, more than ten million people already lived there. These people, now known as Native Americans or American Indians, had lived on the land for thousands of years.

The Indians lived in groups called tribes. Each tribe had its own culture, traditions, language, and history. Some tribes were allies and others were adversaries. They all had ancient roots in the continent that the Europeans wanted to settle.

The United States in 1830

OREGON COUNTRY
(CLAIMED BY BRITAIN
AND THE U.S.)

MICHIGAN TERR.

UNORGANIZED
TERRITORY

MEXICO
(SPANISH TERRITORY)

ARKANSAS
TERR.

ME
VT
NH
MA
NY
RI
CT
PA
NJ
OH
DE
MD
IL   IN
VA
MO
KY
NC
TN
SC
MS   AL   GA
LA
FLORIDA
TERR.

- State
- Territory
- Unorganized territory
- Spanish territory
- Territory claimed by Britain and the U.S.

Over the course of a few centuries, conditions in Europe caused greater numbers of Europeans to seek land in the New World. The populations in European countries grew larger and larger, and land became scarcer. People needed supplies they couldn't get in Europe, like sugar, cotton, tobacco, and lumber. Countries around Europe competed with one another to control trade. They competed by sending their citizens to the New World to start colonies.

These Europeans in North America found themselves in conflict with the people who had lived on the land for generations. In Europe, people bought and sold land. It was owned. The Native Americans did not think of land as property. It belonged to everyone. This difference in viewpoint created misunderstanding, anger, and eventually destruction.

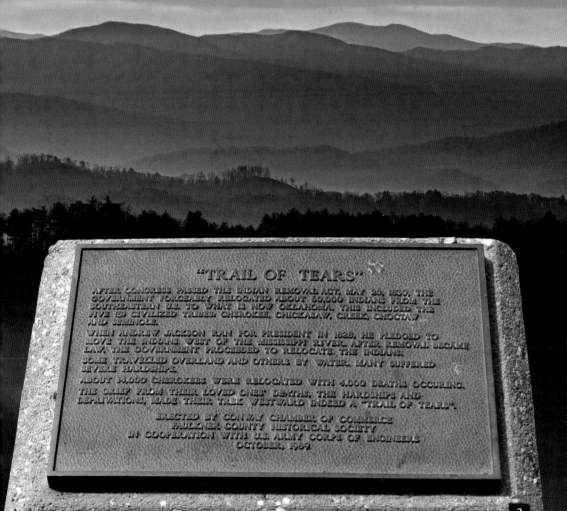

"TRAIL OF TEARS"

AFTER CONGRESS PASSED THE INDIAN REMOVAL ACT, MAY 28, 1830, THE GOVERNMENT FORCEABLY RELOCATED ABOUT 60,000 INDIANS FROM THE SOUTHEASTERN U.S. TO WHAT IS NOW OKLAHOMA. THIS INCLUDED THE FIVE (5) CIVILIZED TRIBES: CHEROKEE, CHICKASAW, CREEK, CHOCTAW AND SEMINOLE.

WHEN ANDREW JACKSON RAN FOR PRESIDENT IN 1828, HE PLEDGED TO MOVE THE INDIANS WEST OF THE MISSISSIPPI RIVER. AFTER REMOVAL BECAME LAW, THE GOVERNMENT PROCEEDED TO RELOCATE THE INDIANS.

SOME TRAVELLED OVERLAND AND OTHERS BY WATER. MANY SUFFERED SEVERE HARDSHIPS.

ABOUT 14,000 CHEROKEES WERE RELOCATED WITH 4,000 DEATHS OCCURING. THE GRIEF FROM THEIR LOVED ONES' DEATHS, THE HARDSHIPS AND DEPRIVATIONS, MADE THEIR TREK WESTWARD INDEED A "TRAIL OF TEARS".

ERECTED BY CONWAY CHAMBER OF COMMERCE
FAULKNER COUNTY HISTORICAL SOCIETY
IN COOPERATION WITH U.S. ARMY CORPS OF ENGINEERS
OCTOBER, 1989

The "Five Civilized Tribes"

When the American Revolution ended in 1783, many white Americans began migrating south to settle. They moved into Georgia, Alabama, North Carolina, Florida, and Tennessee. They wanted rich, fertile land that could be used for growing cotton and other crops.

The Choctaw, Creek, Chickasaw, Cherokee, and Seminole nations already occupied this land. As white settlers arrived, the tribes tried to accommodate them and avoid conflict. They began to farm like Europeans, educate their young like Europeans, speak English, and own slaves. This accommodation earned these American Indians the name the "Five Civilized Tribes."

Despite this attempt at peace, the white settlers often stole the Native Americans' animals, burned their property, and took their land illegally.

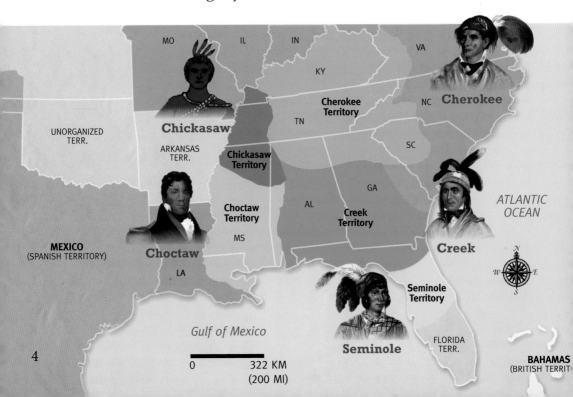

MO   IL   IN   VA

KY

Cherokee
Territory

NC   Cherokee

TN

UNORGANIZED
TERR.

Chickasaw

ARKANSAS
TERR.

Chickasaw
Territory

SC

GA

Choctaw
Territory

AL

Creek
Territory

ATLANTIC
OCEAN

MS

MEXICO
(SPANISH TERRITORY)

Choctaw

Creek

LA

Seminole
Territory

Gulf of Mexico

Seminole

FLORIDA
TERR.

0   322 KM
       (200 MI)

BAHAMAS
(BRITISH TERRIT

During the early 1800s, the U.S. government signed many treaties with the five tribes. Andrew Jackson, an American politician, was integral to many of the treaties. He believed that the tribes should be moved west of the Mississippi River. At that time, few people thought that the United States would ever expand past the river. Those in favor of creating an "Indian Territory" thought that isolation would be good for the Native Americans, giving them space to live as they wanted and govern themselves.

The tribes signed these treaties believing that if they gave some of their ancestral land to the U.S. government, the government would let them stay on a small part of it. However, more and more settlers came and claimed larger tracts of land.

The Indian
Removal Act

In 1829, Andrew Jackson became the seventh president of the United States. The next year he signed the Indian Removal Act, which was labeled "An Act to provide for an **exchange** of lands with the Indians residing in any of the states or territories, and for their removal west of the river Mississippi." It guaranteed that the land the tribes moved to would be theirs forever, unless they left it or became extinct. In return for relocation, the act stipulated that the U.S. government would give the tribes aid for the first year in their new land, and protection for as long as they lived in the designated area.

President Jackson tried to justify removing hundreds of thousands of people from their homes. In his second annual speech to Congress he said, "[The Act] will separate the Indians from immediate contact with settlements of whites . . . [and] enable them to pursue happiness in their own way and under their own rude institutions; will retard the process of decay, which is lessening their numbers, and perhaps cause them gradually, under the protection of the Government and through the influence of good counsels, to cast off their savage habits and become an interesting, civilized, and Christian community."

Origins of the Name "Trail of Tears"

One legend says that a Choctaw chief described the journey to a reporter for the *Arkansas Gazette*. The chief called it "a trail of tears and death." Another story claims that the Cherokee called the journey "the trail where they cried."

Jackson continued, "Doubtless it will be painful to leave the graves of their fathers; but what do they [do] more than our ancestors did or than our own children are now doing? To better their condition in an unknown land our forefathers left all that was dear in earthly objects."

President Jackson wanted the Native Americans to vacate the territories immediately. When they didn't leave on their own, he allowed white settlers to take their land from them. He also used the U.S. Army to force them to leave.

A Voice of Compassion and Reason

Not all white Americans believed the Native Americans should be forced to move. A group of women from Steubenville, Ohio, wrote a petition to Congress in February of 1830. In it they said:

"In despite of the undoubted national right which the Indians have to the land of their forefathers, and in the face of solemn treaties, pledging the faith of the nation for their secure possession of those lands, it is intended, we are told, to force them from their native soil, to compel them to seek new homes in a distant and dreary wilderness. To you, then, as the constitutional protectors of the Indians within our territory, and as the peculiar guardians of our national character, and our country's welfare, we solemnly and honestly appeal, to save this remnant of a much injured people from annihilation, to shield our country from the curses denounced on the cruel and ungrateful, and to shelter the American character from lasting dishonor."

21st CONGRESS,
1st Session.

[Rep. No. 209.]

Ho. OF REPS.

OHIO.

MEMORIAL OF THE LADIES OF STEUBENVILLE, OHIO,

Against the forcible removal of the Indians without the limits of the United States.

FEBRUARY 15, 1830.

Read:—ordered that it lie one day upon the table.

To the Honorable the Senate and House of Representatives of the United States.

Traveling the Trail of Tears

The Treaty of Dancing Rabbit Creek

"The United States . . . shall cause to be conveyed to the Choctaw
Nation a tract of country west of the Mississippi River, in fee simple
to them and their descendants, to inure to them while they shall
exist as a nation and live on it, beginning near Fort Smith, where the
Arkansas boundary crosses the Arkansas River, running thence to
the source of the Canadian fork. . . . The Choctaw nation of Indians
consent and hereby cede to the United States, the entire country
they own and possess, east of the Mississippi River; and they agree to
move beyond the Mississippi River, early as practicable . . ."

The Choctaw Nation

The Choctaw Nation in Mississippi was the first tribe to be completely relocated. The tribal leaders signed the Treaty of Dancing Rabbit Creek on September 27, 1830. This was the first **treaty** signed after the Indian Removal Act was passed. Most of the 23,000 Choctaws **migrated** in three separate groups between 1831 and 1833.

The first group of Choctaws was given two weeks to gather crops and prepare to leave at the beginning of November 1831. The U.S. government promised to give them new livestock in their new land, so animals were left behind. The government also promised gold and a rifle to anyone who walked. Roughly 300 Choctaws took the offer and formed one party. The guide they were given was new to the territory, however, and the group wandered from their path into a swamp. There they got caught in a blizzard.

The other party, led by a U.S. Army escort, hardly fared better. Every encampment they stopped at was unprepared for so many people. There were too few tents, and there was too little food. Many of the children had no clothes. People froze in the cold of winter.

Approximately 6,000 people started the journey in that first group. By the time they reached their new home, only around 4,200 were still alive.

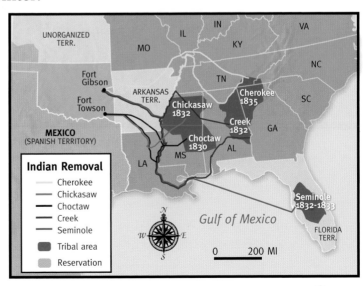

The Creek Nation

In 1832, the Creek chiefs signed the Treaty of Cusseta. The treaty gave their land to the United States, but allowed them to stay on it as residents of the United States if they wished. U.S. government officials hoped that all the Creeks would take the money and land offered in the west, but many of them stayed. Under the treaty, their rights should have been protected in the same way that any U.S. citizen's rights are protected. The government did nothing to protect them, however, allowing white speculators to cheat them out of the land they lived on. Soon the Creeks were **destitute** and desperate. They began raiding white settlements in search of crops and livestock.

Article 12, Treaty of Cusseta, 1832

"The United States are desirous that the Creeks should remove to the country west of the Mississippi, and join their countrymen there; and for this purpose it is agreed, that as fast as the Creeks are prepared to emigrate, they shall be removed at the expense of the United States, and shall receive subsistence while upon the journey, and for one year after their arrival at their new homes—Provided however, that this article shall not be construed so as to compel any Creek Indian to emigrate, but they shall be free to go or stay, as they please."

In 1836, the U.S. Army began to remove the last of the Creeks from their land in Alabama. The Creeks had never signed a **removal treaty**, but the U.S. government now considered them a threat to the safety of the country. Hundreds of the 15,000 Creeks died on the march west. About 3,500 more died from disease, **starvation**, or **malnutrition** after they reached Indian Territory.

The Chickasaw Nation

The Chickasaws lived in northern Mississippi and Alabama. In 1832, they signed a treaty to trade their land for land in Indian Territory. In exchange, they could stay on their land in the south until their representatives found a good place for them in the west. Though they searched, no suitable land was found. Finally, in 1837, the Chickasaws and Choctaws were forced to sign a treaty with the United States that allowed the Chickasaws to rent a part of the Choctaw land in the west.

THE CREEK TRAIL OF TEARS

Approximately one mile due east of this marker, back down the Old Federal Road, called by frontiersmen and Indians the Three Notched Trail or the Three Chopped Way, stood Fort Mitchell, an early 19th century American fort that in 1836 was one of the principal gathering places for the forced removal of the Creek Indians from their homes on the Chattahoochee River to the West. Weakened by starvation, defrauded of their lands and swindled out of most of their possessions, thousands of Creeks, including some in chains and shackles, made the forced journey from Alabama to what is now Oklahoma, where many of their descendants now live. Alabama, also remains the home of many Creek Indians today.

ERECTED BY
THE ALABAMA INDIAN AFFAIRS COMMISSION
AND THE CHATTAHOOCHEE INDIAN HERITAGE ASSOCIATION
1994

From the Memorial of the Creek Nation of Indians

"We beg permission to be left, where your treaties have left us, in the enjoyment of rights as a separate people, and to be treated as unoffending, peaceable inhabitants of our own, and not a borrowed country. . . . May we hope and ask of the Representatives of this great Nation, to deal to our people that measure of justice to which they are entitled, and pledged to them. . ."
—Presented to the Senate and House of Representatives of the United States in Congress assembled, February 1830

11

removal treaty an agreement to abandon the land completely

Between 1836 and 1839, about 5,000 Chickasaws relocated. They took most of their possessions with them. They did not have as many hardships along the Trail of Tears as other tribes, but about 500 Chickasaws died from **smallpox** and malnutrition after they reached Indian Territory. They were tenants on another tribe's land, and this caused a loss of tribal identity.

Article 4, Treaty with the Chickasaws, 1832

"The President being determined that the Chickasaw people shall not deprive themselves of a comfortable home, in the country where they now are, until they shall have provided a country in the west to remove to, and settle on, with fair prospects of future comfort and happiness—It is therefore agreed to, by the Chickasaw nation, that they will endeavor as soon as it may be in their power, after the ratification of this treaty, to hunt out and procure a home for their people, west of the Mississippi river, suited to their wants and condition. . . ."

The Cherokee Nation

The Cherokee lands in northern Georgia and southeastern Tennessee were in danger from the time gold was discovered there in 1828. The Cherokee people were vulnerable to speculators and white miners. The United States wanted their valuable land, and needed them to leave.

In 1835, a small group of Cherokee men signed a treaty with the federal government called the Treaty of New Echota. They were not recognized leaders of the Cherokee Nation, and they had not consulted the tribe, but they agreed to sell all the Cherokee land to the United States for five million dollars and land in Indian Territory. Chief John Ross, the legitimate leader of the tribe, together with more than 15,000 other Cherokees, protested the treaty. They petitioned the **Supreme Court** and Congress to reject the treaty.

Letter from Chief John Ross to the Senate and House of Representatives, 1836

"The instrument in question [Treaty of New Echota] is not the act of our Nation; we are not parties to its covenants; it has not received the sanction of our people. The makers of it sustain no office nor appointment in our Nation, under the designation of Chiefs, Head men, or any other title, by which they hold, or could acquire, authority to assume the reins of Government, and to make bargain and sale of our rights, our possessions, and our common country. . . . Nor can we believe it to be the design of these honorable and highminded individuals, who stand at the head of the Govt., to bind a whole Nation, by the acts of a few unauthorized individuals."

The Supreme Court ruled against the Cherokees. The tribe was given two years to leave **voluntarily**. If they did not leave in those two years, they would be moved by force.

By 1838, 16,000 Cherokees were still on their ancestral land. About 7,000 U.S. Army soldiers marched onto the land and forced them into stockades at gunpoint. They were forced to leave everything behind. John Burnett, a soldier who witnessed the removal, later wrote, "Men working in the fields were arrested and driven to the stockades. Women were dragged from their homes by soldiers whose language they could not understand. Children were often separated from their parents and driven into the stockades with the sky for a blanket and the earth for a pillow. And often the old and infirm were prodded with bayonets to hasten them to the stockades."

Letter from Ralph Waldo Emerson to President Martin Van Buren, 1836

When the writer Ralph Waldo Emerson heard about the plight of the Cherokees, he wrote a letter to the president, urging him to nullify the Treaty of Echota.

"Such a dereliction of all faith and virtue, such a denial of justice, and such deafness to screams for mercy were never heard of in times of peace and in the dealing of a nation with its own allies and wards, since the earth was made. Sir, does this government think that the people of the United States are become savage and mad? From their mind are the sentiments of love and a good nature wiped clean out? The soul of man, the justice, the mercy that is the heart in all men from Maine to Georgia, does abhor this business."

The Cherokees started their 800-mile migration in October of 1838. They faced bitter winter weather, shortages of food and shelter, disease, and the sorrow of being forced away from their home. People died every day, and were buried quickly and anonymously. There was no time to commemorate the dead.

According to Burnett, "The long painful journey to the west ended March 26th, 1839, with four-thousand silent graves reaching from the foothills of the Smoky Mountains to what is known as Indian territory in the West. . . . Somebody must explain the 4,000 silent graves that mark the trail of the Cherokees to their exile. I wish I could forget it all, but the picture of 645 wagons lumbering over the frozen ground with their cargo of suffering humanity still lingers in my memory."

The Seminole Nation

The Seminoles of Florida were fierce, skilled warriors. They had survived in the swamplands of the Everglades for thousands of years. In the early 1800s, Florida was under the control of Spain. The Spanish did not have enough resources to control the Seminoles, and runaway slaves were sheltered with the tribe. The United States fought many wars against the Seminoles during this time. In 1821, Spain ceded Florida to the United States.

A small group of Seminoles in Florida signed the Treaty of Payne's Landing in 1832. The treaty said they would give up their land in Florida and move to Indian Territory. They did not really intend to leave, however. Three years later, the U.S. Army arrived to enforce the treaty, and the Second Seminole War began.

The Seminoles engaged in **guerrilla** warfare against the U.S. military. Small groups of Seminoles ambushed larger groups of soldiers. The Seminoles moved quickly and escaped into the swamps.

Whenever the soldiers captured any Seminoles, they sent them to Indian Territory.

In 1837, Seminole chiefs Osceola and Coacoochee agreed to meet with Thomas Jesup, an army general. They thought they were going to agree to a **truce**, but the general put them both in prison. Osceola died in prison, but Coacoochee escaped. Though many of the Seminoles had been moved to Indian Territory by that time, roughly 300 of them hid away in the swamps, ready to ambush white settlers. No peace treaty was ever signed with the remaining Seminoles, but the war eventually stopped. It had cost the United States 40 to 60 million dollars, and thousands of Seminoles and U.S. soldiers had died.

Conclusion

By 1840, more than 46,000 Native Americans had traveled along the Trail of Tears. More than twenty-five million acres of Native American land was taken over by the white settlers, and the government continued to break the promises it made in the Indian Removal Act. Many people consider this time to be a devastating moment in American history.

The forced migration of Native Americans to "Indian Territory" in Oklahoma was completed by 1842. Thousands of people died on what is now known as the Trail of Tears.

When they arrived in this new territory, each of the Five Civilized Tribes became its own nation. Each tribe had its own government and constitution. They also had their own homes, schools, and land to farm. A series of events, however, led to further loss of their lands and independence.

When the Civil War broke out in 1861, the Union government in the North pulled out its troops from Indian Territory, which was close to the Confederate states in the South. The tribes were left on their own. Two of the tribes, the Choctaw and Chickasaw, supported the Confederacy. The other three tribes had troops on both sides, though the Cherokee favored the Union.

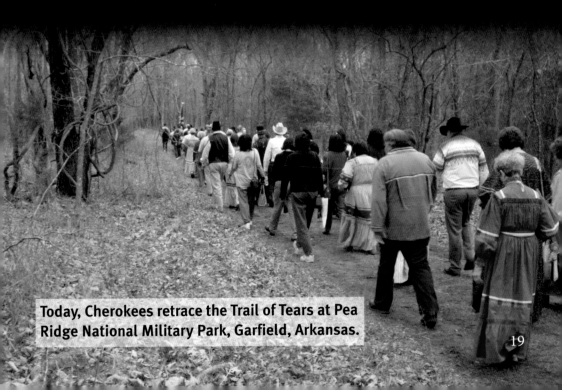

Today, Cherokees retrace the Trail of Tears at Pea Ridge National Military Park, Garfield, Arkansas.

At the end of the war, the U.S. government decided that new treaties with the tribes had to be written. The United States claimed that the Indians had given up their rights under their old treaties because they had supported the Confederacy during the war. The government did not acknowledge that many Indians fought for the North. As a result, each of the tribes had to give up sizable tracts of land to the United States. Altogether, it amounted to the western half of what is now Oklahoma.

More loss of Indian Territory followed in the late 1800s. White Americans who wanted to move west were putting pressure on the U.S. government to make Indian lands available for settlement. This led to the Land Rush of 1885 and the Land Rush of 1889, which opened up millions of acres of tribal land to white settlers. By 1905, these settlers owned most of the Indian Territory.

In 1907, the state of Oklahoma (a Choctaw word meaning "red people") was established, combining the Indian Territory with the Oklahoma Territory.

Today, there are thirty-nine tribal governments in the United States. Thirty-eight of them are federally recognized tribes and tribal towns in Oklahoma. These tribes continue to preserve their culture, community, and heritage.

Children receive prizes at a dance competition at the annual Red Earth festival in Oklahoma City.

About the Indian Removal Act

Now that you have read about the Trail of Tears, let's read three writers' opinions about the removal of the Native Americans from their lands and their journey along the Trail of Tears. Each writer was given the same writing prompt, highlighted below. The writers have written from different points of view, and each has a different opinion, yet each essay provides a good example of writing a strong argument. A well-written argument is backed up by reasons, uses transition words, and has a concluding statement. In the first opinion piece, annotations have been added to help you identify these important parts of an opinion piece.

Opinion Writing Prompt

Imagine that you are from one of the Native American tribes affected by the Indian Removal Act. Write a letter to President Andrew Jackson. State which group you are from. Tell why you are opposed to the act. Defend your opinion using evidence from the text.

Letter from a Cherokee Indian

To the Honorable President Jackson:

The writer begins with a clearly stated opinion.

The writer creates an organizational structure that lists reasons for the opinion.

The writer uses linking words to connect opinions and response.

   I am writing to you as a Cherokee and a member of one of the Five Civilized Tribes. In the name of our people, I must protest your decision to sign the Indian Removal Act. It is unjust. It is wrong for the U.S. government to force the Cherokees from their native lands. For the following reasons, I ask that you reconsider this decision and allow us to remain on our homelands.

   <u>First</u>, your Indian Removal Act of 1830 is based on untrue claims. In your address to Congress, you said, "Doubtless it will be painful to leave the graves of their fathers; but what do they [do] more than our ancestors did . . .? To better their condition in an unknown land our forefathers left all that was dear in earthly objects." It is unfair to compare our situation to that of your forefathers. They chose to leave their homeland, using their own free will. Our people do not have a choice. Rather, we are being forced to leave our homes and lands by the U.S. government.

It is also not true that we are leaving these lands to better our condition as your forefathers did. We have lived here for thousands of years and many generations. We have a rich history with many cultures and traditions. We have farmed our lands wisely and productively. Why would we seek to "better our condition"? The Indian Removal Act demands that we move to unknown wilderness far from our homes. The first of our tribes to be relocated, the Choctaws, lost many of their people on the journey west. With little food and no shelter, hundreds froze to death. Are these the better conditions you promise our people when we leave our homelands?

Also, Mr. President, we have done nothing that should cause you to take our lands. When the white settlers first came to these lands from the North, our people welcomed them. We did not want conflict with our white neighbors. We tried to share the abundance of the land. We even adopted many of your people's ways. Our children are educated and we speak the white man's language. We have even adopted your religious practices. It is for these reasons that we have been called one of the "Civilized Tribes."

> The writer uses evidence from the text to support a reason.

> The writer continues to use linking words to connect opinions and reasons.

The writer continues to use evidence from the text to support a reason.

But your people took our land, which did not belong to them. They burned our property, and stole our animals. In addition, when the settlers also became greedy for gold, your government did not protect us. The profits from the gold should have been ours. But your government did not agree. You let the miners invade our property. They stole our gold, and gave us nothing in return. Neither the federal government nor the state of Georgia came to our aid. The greedy miners took away our wealth and our homes. Your people are invaders, Sir, and you have no right to tell us where we can live.

The writer continues to use evidence from the text to support a reason.

Still another reason your decision is unjust is because the treaty you signed with members of our tribe does not represent what the Cherokees want. The three Cherokee men who signed a treaty with your government in 1835 were not our chosen leaders. They had not even consulted with our true leader, Chief John Ross, who did not sign the treaty. In a letter to the Senate and House of Representatives, Chief Ross said, "The instrument in question [Treaty of Echota] is not the act of our Nation; . . . it has not received the sanction of our people." He even appealed to your Supreme Court to reject the fake treaty. But the protest had no effect. Your court approved the treaty, going against thousands of Cherokees who protested.

Mr. President, have you listened to your own people? I am glad to know that not every American citizen has become cruel and uncivilized. I have seen political cartoons in newspapers. I have read the petition of the women from Steubenville, Ohio, who asked Congress to save the Indians from "annihilation" and to "shelter the American character from lasting dishonor." These citizens are correct. Your reputation as a nation will be harmed by your actions toward the Native Americans. Who will ever again believe that the United States is the land of the free?

The writer continues to use evidence from the text to support a reason.

Now you are forcing our people out of our homes and into stockades. Can you imagine, even for a moment, the grief our people feel? We can only watch as your settlers steal our goods, take over our land, and move into our homes. I only wish you could hear the weeping and wailing of our people as we flee.

The writer provides a concluding statement or section.

You have told Congress that we must cast off our savage habits. Who is the savage, Sir? Is it us, or is it the government stealing money and property, banishing a race of people to a harsh, foreign wilderness?

Letter from a Seminole Indian

Dear Mr. President:

As a woman of the Seminole Nation, I plead with you. Do not force us to leave our native lands in Florida and march west to unknown territories. You say that removing us from our homes will enable us to pursue happiness in our own way. You say that forcing us to make this journey will "slow the decay" of our tribes, which is lessening our numbers. But the opposite is true. The journey will instead force our decline and decimation, and the United States will suffer great losses.

As the president of a civilized nation, would you treat your own families this way? Would you force your own grandfather off of the land his family had lived on for generations? Would you force your own children to walk hundreds of miles with no shoes or proper provisions?

The journey you are asking us to make is longer than 800 miles, and we are told we must walk the entire way. Such a move will kill our people in spirit, and many of us in body. Our elders and our sick ones will never make it. Mothers will struggle to carry babies. Many will surely die along the way.

Other tribes that have gone before us have suffered great losses. More than 1,000 Choctaws, many of them young children, froze to death as they journeyed west. Hundreds of the Creek Nation also died on the march to new land—and 3,000 more died after they reached Indian Territory. They suffered from disease, starvation, and malnutrition. The journey will not slow the decay of our tribes, as you say, but hasten it.

Further, if the Seminoles are forced from our home, you will lose many American soldiers. Our nation has survived in the Everglades for thousands of years, and I assure you that we will not go quietly or easily. The U.S. military has already engaged in many wars with our fierce warriors. If we are forced off our land, there will be another war with many losses on both sides. Too many of us, and too many of your soldiers, have already died in past conflicts. Another war will cost you dearly, in both lives and money.

Please, too much blood has already been spilled. There is still time for your government to work out a truce with Chief Osceola and our other leaders. Please reconsider our forced removal. For the sake of our young and elderly, and your own lives, do not relocate us to a strange land.

Letter from a Creek Indian

Dear Mr. President:

I echo the words of Ralph Waldo Emerson when I say that never in the history of the world has there been such a denial of justice. He spoke of the Cherokees. I speak of the Creeks. Our situations are different, but our plight is the same. Though we were promised protection by the United States, we are being driven off our lands by our white neighbors. We face destitution, cheated out of our land and homes. Are we now to be forced off our ancestral lands like the Creeks and other tribes, in spite of your pledge? As residents of your civilized nation, do we not have rights the same as any other citizen?

When we signed the Treaty of Cusseta, it was stated that no Creek would be compelled to leave our land. Our treaty was a compromise—we gave our land with the provision we could remain as residents. We were "free to go or stay" as we pleased. But your government has done nothing to protect our rights as inhabitants of this land. White speculators have invaded our remaining territory, and they have cheated us. We have no more resources. In order to survive, we have been forced to steal from the very homesteads we ourselves once owned.

Before we found ourselves destitute, we were fair neighbors to the white settlers. We always abided by the terms of our treaties. We allowed speculators on our ancestral land, and shared resources with them in the hope of enjoying the rights of a peaceful, independent people. We signed the Treaty of Cusseta hoping to maintain this status. We want to live on our own land, not borrowed land, even if we are given only a small piece of it. But none of these appeasements have satisfied our white neighbors. You offer us money to get out of their way, but all we want is to be left on our own.

You have caused the problems your white settlers now face. By failing to protect our rights as you promised, you have allowed speculators to cheat us of land and resources. You have violated the terms of our agreement, leaving us no choice but to take back what is rightfully ours in order to survive. You thought you could bribe us to leave, but we won't accept it. We want our land more than your money. We've kept our part of the bargain. Now it's time for you to keep yours. Honor the terms of the Treaty of Cusseta. As the Memorial of the Creek Nation of Indians, addressed to your Congress, put forth, we ask your Nation "to deal to our people that measure of justice to which they are entitled, and pledged to them."

Evaluate the Opinion Texts

Opinion Writing Rubric				
Opinion Trait	**4**	**3**	**2**	**1**
The writer states a strong opinion, position, or point of view.				
The writer supplies well-organized reasons that support his or her opinion using facts, concrete examples, and supporting evidence from the text.				
The writer links opinions and reasons using words, phrases, and clauses.				
The writer provides a concluding statement or section that supports the position.				

4—exemplary; 3—accomplished; 2—developing; 1—beginning

Glossary

destitute   (DES-tih-toot) *adjective* extremely poor; particularly suffering from lack of food, clothing, and shelter (page 10)

exchange   (iks-CHANJE) *noun* a trade of things of similar value (page 6)

guerrilla   (guh-RIH-luh) *adjective* referring to a style of fighting in which fighters use surprise attacks (page 17)

malnutrition   (mal-noo-TRIH-shun) *noun* a sickness caused by eating food that is not healthful or by not eating enough food (page 11)

migrated   (MY-gray-ted) *verb* moved from one area to another to live (page 9)

smallpox   (SMAUL-pahks) *noun* a contagious disease (page 12)

starvation   (star-VAY-shun) *noun* the state of not having enough food (page 11)

Supreme Court   (suh-PREEM KORT) *noun* the highest court that hears legal cases in the United States; it has nine judges who are appointed by the president (page 13)

treaty   (TREE-tee) *noun* a written agreement between two groups or countries (page 9)

truce   (TROOS) *noun* an agreement to stop fighting (page 18)

voluntarily   (vah-lun-TAIR-ih-lee) *adverb* by choice (page 14)

Analyze the Text

Questions for Close Reading

Use facts and details from the text to support your answers to the following questions.

- Describe the treaty that was signed by the Creek Nation in 1832. What was the relationship like between the Creek Nation and the settlers after this treaty was signed?

- Why did Chief John Ross and thousands of Cherokees disagree with the treaty that was signed in 1835?

- Reread paragraph 7 in Opinion 1. What evidence did the writer provide to support the statement that some white settlers objected to the Indian Removal Act?

- Reread the conclusion of Opinion 3. What evidence does the writer provide to support the statement "We've kept our part of the bargain. Now it's time for you to keep yours."

Distinguish and Evaluate Fact and Opinion

The writers of the opinion essays give their opinions about the Indian Removal Act and provide factual evidence from the text to support their opinions and reasons. Choose one of the opinion essays. Use a chart to list three opinion statements and three factual pieces of evidence from the essay. Then, tell how each statement supports the writer's main opinion.

Facts	Opinions
1.	1.
2.	2.
3.	3.